This book belongs to:

COPYRIGHT © 2019 BY TRICIA HARRELL.
ALL RIGHTS RESERVED.

YOU CAN CONTACT TRICIA HARRELL AT
INFO@STARLIGHTPRESSBYTRICIA.COM
INSTAGRAM: @STARLIGHTPRESSBYTRICIA
FACEBOOK: STARLIGHTPRESSBYTRICIA

Ava is a young girl who is fascinated by aquatic animals. She fell in love with sea creatures after her grandmother brought a book about a young ocean explorer.

This book told fascinating stories about a girl who loved to explore the great, big world under the sea.

From that day, Ava decided that she wants to be a Marine Biologist when she grows up. Someone who studies sea creatures.

Sunday
21

Because she loves the ocean animals, she gets excited
when her dad takes her to the Aquarium.

Every Sunday, Ava's dad would take her to the Aquarium
to see the sea creatures.

Today is Sunday, and Ava is eagerly waiting to go to the
Aquarium. The Aquarium opened at 11:00 a.m., but Ava
could not wait any longer. She thought that 11:00 a.m.
was too far away.

Ava's dad saw that she looked very sad. He said, "Let's
play a game." In this game, Ava and her dad must name
one sea animal for every letter in the alphabet.

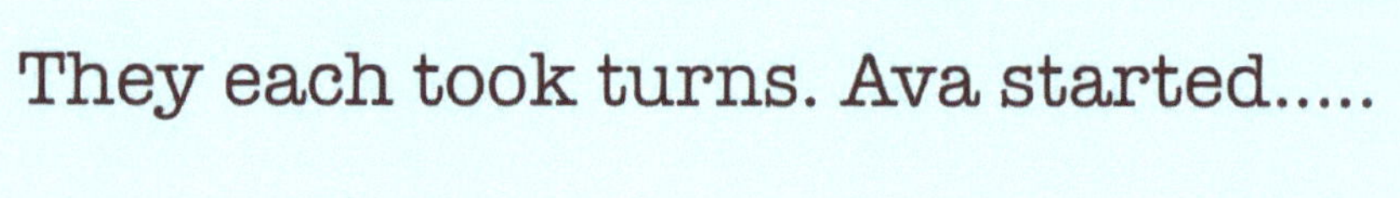

They each took turns. Ava started.....

C is for Clown
fish

B is for Beluga
Whale

A is for Angel
fish

D is for
Dolphin

E is for
Eel

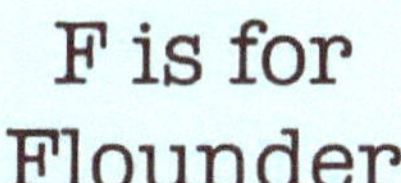

F is for
Flounder

Sunday
21
Hooray!
Hooray!

As the game went on, they lost track of time. "Oh, no!
It's almost time to go," said Dad.

Ava jumped in joy. "Hooray! Hooray!"

Ava rushed to her room and put on her favorite clothes.
She ran out of her room and into her father's arms,
yelling, "Please drive fast, daddy. I cannot wait to get
to the Aquarium!"

Dolphin show
Ticket Counter

At the Aquarium, Ava gave the desk clerk her ticket.
The desk clerk buzzed it through the automatic ticket
checking machine.

Ava loved how the ticket checking machine sounded
(Buzzzzzzzzzz...Buzzzzzzzzzzz...) as they entered.

It was a sign that they were in the Aquarium and free
to explore!

"Have a nice day, young lady," said the desk clerk as
Ava and her dad went through the turnstile.
Ava replied with a smile, "Thank you. You have a nice
day too."

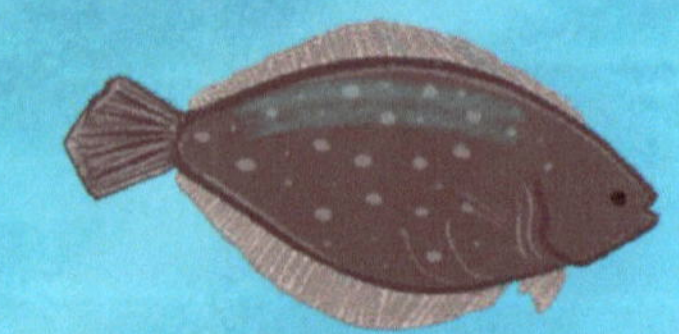

"Look, daddy," said Ava pointing at the sea turtle hiding in its shell.

"Do you know that sea turtles are known as ancient creatures?" asked daddy. "No," replied Ava.

"They are creatures that have been on Earth for a very long time," said daddy.

"Daddy, are the turtles older than the dinosaurs?"

Daddy laughed and said, "These turtles are not older than the dinosaurs, Ava."

Ava learned more fun facts from her dad about the beautiful creatures that they saw.

They saw starfish, clownfish, sea turtles, whales,
and a shark.

They continued to explore the Aquarium until daddy
checked his watch and said, "Oops! We are late!"

Ava looked up at her father and said, "What are we late for, daddy? Do we have to go home already?" Daddy said, "I have a little surprise for you. Come with me."

Ava held onto her father's hand and walked as fast as she could. When she noticed that they were walking toward the theater, Ava's eyes lit up with excitement.

She looked at her father and said, "Daddy! Are we going to watch the show today?"

Daddy smiled at Ava and said, "Yes, honey."

19

The show only happened once a month, and Ava loved to watch the show. This is where Ava saw her favorite sea animal, the dolphin, doing tricks with a ball on its nose.

"Look, Daddy," said Ava. "The dolphin is balancing the ball on his nose just like the curious clown."

"Yes, he is!" said daddy.

Ava and her dad watched in amazement as the dolphin leaped and spun.

After the show, Ava and her dad walked around some more. Ava pretended like she was walking at the bottom of the sea. She wondered what it would be like to swim with the dolphins.

She looked at her dad and said, "Daddy, can I swim with the dolphins?"
Daddy looked down at Ava and said, "I don't think so, honey."

Just then, Ray, the caretaker of the dolphins, walked up to them and said, "Sir, we do allow children to enter the pool with the dolphins."

Ray is a college student who also loves dolphins. He volunteers at the Aquarium during his holidays.
Ava's eyes lit up with excitement. She looked at her dad with pleading eyes.

Daddy said, "Oh well! You can swim with the dolphins but on one condition. You must listen to this man here."
Ava looked earnestly at her daddy and said, "Yes, daddy. I promise to listen to everything that he says."

The dolphins swam really close to Ava. She could even reach them. Ava had so much fun playing with the dolphins. She did not want to get out of the water.

Ray looked at Ava and said, "Time's up, Ava. We must come out of the water now. Your father will be waiting for us." Ava remembered the promise she made to her father and stepped out of the pool with Ray.

After her swim with the dolphins, Ava was tired and ready to go home.

When they got home, Ava rushed out of the car and ran to her mother.

She said, "Mommy! Mommy! I had the best day at the Aquarium today! Do you know what I got to do?"
Mommy said, "What was it, honey?"

Ava said, "I swam with the dolphins! I was not scared of swimming in the deep!"
Mommy said, "Ava, that is lovely! I am proud of you."

Ava went on and on about the beautiful things she had learned and seen at the Aquarium. She walked into the kitchen with her mother and continued to tell her about her day.

Ava's mom prepared one of Ava's favorite dishes—spaghetti and meatballs.
Ava sat at the dinner table and continued to talk about her day while eating.
"Yummy!" said Ava as she took the last bite of her meal.

Sunday
21

After dinner, she brushed her teeth and changed into her pajamas to head to bed.

Mommy and daddy came to tuck her in. "Can you read me this book?" asked Ava, pointing to the book on the bookshelf.

Mom picked up the book and read the story until Ava drifted off to sleep, dreaming about the incredible day she had at the Aquarium with her dad..